Dead Before 18

Saving Our Boys From The Streets

Written by Lamont Carey

Edited by

Melanee Woodard

Libra Mayo

Miranda Sherill

Book design and graphics Created by

J. P. Lago

Photo of Lamont Carey taken by

April Sims Photography

Vol.1 Dead Before 18

Copyright © 2016 by Lamont Carey

Twitter: @lamontcarey

Facebook: LaCareyentertainment,llc/lamontcarey

Distributed Worldwide

ISBN-13: 978-1-945806-00-1

ISBN-10:1-945806-00-1

Special Thanks

Special thanks to Pharaoh, Melanee Woodard, Libra, Lady Flava, Holli Holliday, Robert Carey, Jacqueline Boles, Jermaine Ingram, Horace Ellis, Fred Chandler, Meryl Ironson, Joseph Pizzo, Hermond Palmer, Mark Holden, Jona Vandeun, Jenny Kim, Clinton Lacey, Tyrone Hicks,Drew Anderson, Rahiem Jenkins, Michelle Parker, Christine Graham, Genine Hagar, Margaret Quick, Angelyn Frazier, Rep. Laura Hall, Rep. Helen Miller, Catherine Pugh, Brenda Richardson, Sherry Washington, Mira Sherill, Sharon Coker, Stinky Dink, NOBLE WOMEN, Women In Government, Aneika Saabira, Tina Kennedy, Heather E. Strachan, Carolyn Saxon, Mary Brown, Charles Mitchell, Dyone Mitchell, April Sampe, Allie Bird, Bro. Rob, Lakeal Ellis, Bianca Brown, Dee Pasha, Maka Taylor, my family, my social media network family, my supporters, and any and everyone I forgot.

Table of Contents

Dear Reader:

Thanks for giving my book a chance. My hope is to give you some insight from my observations and personal experiences as a youth and adult. I grew up in poverty. I hated that place and the people. I wanted out and I didn't care how I got out. I felt limited because I didn't like school and I was told that even if I graduated that I wouldn't be anything. My father was a heroin addict and hustler. He died when I was 10 years old. To tell you the truth, I hated the man because he abused my mother. How he treated her made me declare that NO ONE would ever get over on me. In a nutshell, that was all that I knew about my father and the impression he left on me. So before he died, I was already a knucklehead little boy. When he died, I stepped up my fighting and began bullying dudes. Soon, I was selling drugs, dropped out of school, started using guns and at the age of 16, I was charged as an adult and sent to an adult prison.

That's a little bit about me. I wrote this book because I wanted to have the conversation with you that I wish someone would have had with me. I'll be sharing with you what I know about the streets, school and gangs. I will also talk about young guys thinking and trying to become a man in this complicated world we live in. I plan to keep it 100 with you and I only ask that you keep it 100 with yourself as you read.

Men Don't Cry

Boys are told so many things about what boys should or shouldn't do. The first thing on the list, don't cry. Has somebody ever said this to you, "Stop crying", "Boys don't cry", "Be a man", "Stop acting like a punk", "You're crying for no reason" or "You're a cry baby"? For some reason people tell us that it's not manly to be emotional and young boys interpret that to mean men are never supposed to show tears. And if you consider yourself a man in the making, you stop crying. You go even further and stop showing any pain, fear and even doubt. Regardless of all the drama and disappointment that affects us, we are supposed to act like we don't care and it doesn't bother us. We start saying stuff like, "I'm good." "I'm alright." "I don't care." And my favorite, "I ain't tripping." Our arm can be dangling and half ripped from our body and the ambulance worker can be asking, "are you okay", and we are liable to say, "Yea. I'm good." We begin to believe if we admit that we feel any kind of pain, we are somehow less than a man and weak. So when something happens that hurts us, we usually try to play it off or act tough.

Another example: have you ever been playing rough and you hit the back of your elbow (your funny bone) on something and that tingling pain shoots through your arm? That stuff hurts! Did people start shouting for you to walk it off? What did you do? You probably winced in pain but held the pain in and tried to walk it off! You mumbled through clenched teeth, "I'm alright. I'm good."

They taught me that as well. So, I didn't cry in front of anyone. If I felt like the tears were going to betray me and fall out of my eyes, I would turn my head or walk away. You can't say I am crying if you don't hear the whining or see the tears. Nothing was going to make me less than a man. So I grew up not showing any kind of pain.

Another problem that boys and men have, is that we take it to mean that we are not supposed to be fearful of anything or anyone. Even when we don't want to fight, we fight because if we don't, we're not a man. Or we start daring each other to do stupid stuff to prove we're not scared and that we're men. "I bet you won't kick that car door. I bet you won't walk on that fence. I bet you won't steal that candy bar. I bet you won't punch that dude. Oh, you heard what so and so said about you and your momma, what you going to do? You scared?" We become so fearful of being labeled a chicken, a sucker, a punk or a sissy, that we literally destroy our lives sometimes.

While in prison I learned that a boy that doesn't cry, will never truly be a man. He's too busy living a lie and hiding from himself. Boys feel pain. Men hurt too. If you weren't supposed to cry, you wouldn't feel anything. Those of us who are taught that little boys don't cry, don't even cry when we're happy.

We live in a world where things don't always go our way and sometimes that hurts. Our body shows our disappointment and sadness through tears and we deny ourselves of that. When was the last time you cried? When was the last time you wanted to cry?

Look, you have been lied to. I have been lied to. Maybe they told us that because our crying was getting on their nerves. Maybe they taught us that because that's what they were taught. All I can tell you is that they were wrong. The worst thing you can do to yourself is live your life like nothing bothers you. It will surely cause you to do things you don't want to do because you don't want to show any fear. It's time for you to live your life and to stop walking around as if nothing bothers you. You're not a machine so you are not heartless.Stop saying, it's whatever. You're a good dude. Don't let no one turn you into a monster.

Ain't Nothing Wrong With Me. I'm Good

The streets taught me that I should keep everybody out of my business. If you asked me how I was feeling, I would immediately say, "I'm good." Just saying, "I'm good," is like a wall of protection that dudes build to keep everyone from knowing what's really going on with them. Have you ever heard that saying, "A closed mouth doesn't get fed"? It basically means if you never tell anyone what you want or need, you may never get it. I remember I used to say, "I'm good" all the time even when I was really going through something. I didn't want to talk about it because I didn't want to come off as soft, whining or complaining. I told myself that I could handle it. I'll figure it out on my own. Most of the dudes I knew did the same thing. We all ended up making the situation worse or never received the answers or the help we needed.

Thinking like that has literally played a part in dudes losing their lives, getting locked up or caused more suffering. You are probably like, "How?" Let's say that you got into a fight with someone that you know is going to come back with his boys or a weapon. After the fight, you go into the house with a look of worry on your face and your mom notices. She asks you what is going on and you reply, "I'm good." Then you get up and leave the house because she is going to keep trying to find out what's wrong. So, you walk out and right into the drama you were worried about. The dude has a weapon or his boys are with him and you start fighting. You lose the fight and your life on the other side of the door where she is and she doesn't even know it. If you had told her about the fight earlier and your thoughts on the dude coming back, she wouldn't have let you walk out that house. She could have helped you figure out a solution to this problem. Instead you walked right into the drama.

You can't solve all of your problems alone. We all need guidance and help. It doesn't make you a punk to get some advice from someone who can help you. Plus, the situation doesn't have to be as extreme as the example I just gave you. My point is, if you are constantly saying, "I'm good" when you're not, you might create a bigger problem for yourself. You don't know everything and there is nothing wrong with asking for some guidance or getting a second opinion.

I was forced to learn that most of us that find ourselves getting into fights constantly, running from the police constantly, getting locked up constantly, being kicked out of our home constantly and even getting killed, suffer from the "Ain't nothing wrong with me, I'm good" syndrome. Why that hurts us more than anything is because we don't feel comfortable asking for help, assistance, support or whatever you want to call it. We go about our lives trying to figure everything out on our own. I'm not sure if that's because people haven't kept their word with us, let us down, left us or just mistreated us, so we say, "from here on out, I'ma make it on my own". Most of the time that means we're going to get it "anywhere" or "anyway we can." And that usually translates into stealing it, snatching it, selling something for it or killing somebody to get it. "Anyway we can," doesn't become the solution, it becomes a bigger problem for us.

Just think about it, what was the reason you said, "I'm good," when you really wasn't? Were you just trying to keep people out of your business, or you thought they would think less of you? How did you resolve the issue?

Look, we all go through hard times. I'm not saying that your situation isn't different than everyone else's, I'm just saying that a solution to the problem exists. Somebody else can help you solve this problem, whatever it is. I'm not telling you to go run your mouth to everybody who asks,"are you ok?" I'm just saying you have to learn to trust somebody. Just make sure that somebody is a person you believe makes good decisions and not a fool who is going to make your situation worse than it already is. The goal is to solve the problem with the best outcome.

Find someone you can trust. They don't always have to be able to solve your problem. It could just be someone who is willing to listen. A lot of times I have resolved my issues just by being able to talk about it and I come up with the answer.

I can't stress this enough. I want you to win at life. No one is successful by themselves. If you never ask for help, you may never receive it and you may never get whatever it is that you want.

My Anger

Have you ever been frustrated to the point where you just wanted to punch or kick something or someone and you didn't even know why you were feeling that way? I'm talking about one of those days where you told yourself, I just want somebody to say something stupid and we're going to war! Have you had one of those days and you meant it? You didn't even know why you were mad. You didn't even try to find out why you were mad. You were just ready to fight anything. Have you ever felt like that?

I've felt that way many times when I was a youngster. I didn't understand why I was feeling that way but I got what I was looking for. Either someone said something or looked at me in a way that I used to turn into a fight or I intentionally annoyed someone until they reacted in a way that I could justify punching them in the face. Did it make me feel better? It probably did for a few minutes, but only if they ran away after I hit them. If you have done this before, I'm sure afterwards, you kept looking over your shoulders every time someone or a car came in your direction. You stayed on alert because you were expecting them to return with family members, friends or with a weapon. You also started worrying about the police coming to arrest you. That whole day you walked around on high alert. The problem is, it never addressed why you were having a bad day in the first place. So, now that feeling is gone and replaced with the fear of retaliation or arrest.

That feeling went away too, once nothing happened after a few hours. The next time you wake up wanting to fight, you'll probably hit someone because you think it is the cure to your bad day and it appears to be no repercussions. The issue with that is you will keep doing it and never try to figure out why you're irritated. The other problem is...you never think about all of your victims. You start to think those punks are scared of me and they don't want to see me again. In your mind, you start to believe you'll crush anybody and you'll fight anybody, young, old, short or tall. Anybody can get it if they want it and you'll keep swinging on people until someone beats the breaks off of you or someone kills you. That's what happens to folks who become bullies unless you realize that you can't keep taking your frustrations out on people.

There are a few things that I want you to remember:

1. Taking your frustration out on people never solves your real problems.

2. People never forget bullies especially those that beat them up.

3. One day the police will come to arrest you either for assault or murder. I'm sure you are aware that you can hit someone and not know that they have health problems and your punch kills them. Or you hit somebody so hard that their head hits the ground and it kills them. Now, you end up in prison with more frustrations and urges to swing on some one. In prison, they will swing back. The only difference is that they may have a knife in their clenched fist when they are swinging.

If you don't believe that you can hit someone and kill them, google it. You'll discover it happens and the person that did the hitting ends up in prison for a very long time, if not for the rest of their lives. It doesn't matter if you are a juvenile when you accidentally killed the person because the court's charge juveniles as adults all the time. Some as young as 11 years old have been charged as adults and sent to prison. Remember all of this started because you woke up in a bad mood and you took your bad mood out on somebody who had nothing to do with how you were feeling.

When you have a chance, look up school shootings online and read why most of the people said they killed and shot people at the schools. You'll discover that the majority of the young shooters were being bullied. I'm not trying to scare you. I wouldn't waste our time with that. I just want to make sure you're aware of the consequences for the choices you're making. See how we keep coming back to the consequences of your actions?

Let's look at some possible reasons why you may be waking up frustrated or why you may become easily irritated:

1. It could be a very hot day and your body is overheating. Try to drink some cool water or go

to a room where there are air conditioners blowing to see if that changes your mood.

2. You could be hungry and not even realize it. So, try to eat something even if it is a snack and monitor if your mood changes.

3. Maybe you have a school test, job interview or getting ready to start something new. Your frustration can really be nervousness which is typical. I would suggest you review what you have been studying to make yourself more comfortable with taking the test. This way you know you are prepared. If it is a new school, I think you should remind yourself that you're going to make a lot of new friends. Some of those will be cool new guys and pretty new females. You're going to make a new best friend and have tons of fun. Plus, you're going to have some new learning experiences.

4. You had an argument with somebody you care about so you really don't want to see them because the argument can begin again. That could be making you uncomfortable. I would suggest revisiting the argument in your mind. If

you were wrong, admit it and apologize. If you didn't say things the way you wanted to, apologize and explain it the way you meant to before the argument started. If the person was wrong, ask them if the two of you could talk and calmly explain it to them again. Also, I have had arguments that I have gotten over immediately but I still acted like I was still mad because the person still seemed mad. That keeps the tension high and the potential for another disagreement. You have to figure out how to end feuds.

5. You feel powerless in your home because you're told to do things you don't want to do or you feel your opinion isn't important. One way you can address that is when the other person(s) seems to have calmed down, you can politely ask to have a conversation with them. Just explain how you feel, and why you feel that way. It may help the situation. If you have tried this and it hasn't worked, just start doing whatever it is that you have been asked to do before you're asked to do it. Put yourself on a schedule. For example, if they don't want you on the phone after 7pm then you need to

schedule your phone calls with your friends before that time. If the problem is taking out the trash, it may be easier to take out the trash before you take your shower or when you leave the house in the morning, that way, you don't have to take it out at night. If the arguing is about you doing homework, start doing some of your homework at school so you won't have a lot to do when you get home. There is a solution to every problem. You just have to think it through and figure out how to get what you want and give them what they want. You have to make it a win-win situation.

Another thing that I do when I am frustrated is shadow boxing. Shadow boxing is throwing punches at your shadow. I will go somewhere like in my bedroom or out back and just box my shadow or throw punches at the air. I would pretend like I am boxing someone for three minute rounds. I mean, I would act like I am getting hit and everything. I'll be throwing jabs, hooks, uppercuts and pushing my opponent off of me when I am getting the best of him. I act like I am blocking his jabs, hitting him when he is trying to grab me or I would grab him if he is getting the best of me. I would take a thirty second break and then go right back to shadow boxing. Trust me, this works. You will release a lot of anger. Plus, it's a workout! I'm telling you, try this when you're frustrated. My biggest suggestion with shadowboxing, do this where no one can see you. If you do it in front of people, people will want to join in and box you and that can turn into a fight. I suggest you go jogging and shadow box on a bridge, down a street but not in front of your friends or in front of someone that may want to test you. You're doing this to get rid of the frustration and not to start a war. It also works great with headphones on or put the radio on and just get lost in your favorite music.

One of the other things I learned to do when I got frustrated at school was recite my favorite rap songs in my head. I wouldn't beat on the school desk or say it out loud because someone would say something and now I am ready to fight. I would just rock my head to the beat in my head and just recite the rap in my thoughts. My eyes would be glistening with frustration and I would ride those emotions. If I want to calm down faster I would sing my favorite love song in the same way I would rap. The love song always changed my mood. Music, for some reason, has a way of calming me down, even if it is a rap or a song that I am making up in my head. You might want to try this in school or anywhere. It helps.

Another thing that I do is go for a walk through a park or wooded area. Now, I am not a religious guy but I would have conversations with God or one of my dead buddies or relatives. I would complain or ask for help. I would converse like they were there. I even used to call God "Slim". Sometimes I would be so mad or hurt about something that I cried. The point is that I got what was on my mind out. I was dealing with the issue in my own way. The reason I used to go to the park or a wooded area is so that no one would see me. I didn't have to worry about being judged.

One of the last things that I learned to do is find a friend who I could confide in. I was very cautious about that because friendships can end. I couldn't choose a friend that would put my business in the street. So I started evaluating my friends to see which ones would keep my secrets. I ended up with two friends who I still trust to this day. Either one I could turn to and tell them the way I feel and why. Sometimes I thought their advice would work for me and it did. Other times it didn't work. Sometimes I knew it wouldn't work so I didn't even try it. The bigger point is that I found someone I could tell "my secrets" to. Whether I felt their advice would work for me or not, it felt better to just talk about it. I was so used to trying to figure it out by myself. Sometimes, I walked away from my friends saying to myself, "Man, he has lost his mind." I would end up laughing and that made it feel even better.

In the end, I learned not to fight or try to hurt someone to stop my feelings of frustration and anger. I suggest you try any if not all of them and let me know if it works for you.

Impulsive Behavior

Impulsivity is a tendency to act without thinking about the consequences of your actions. These actions usually occur in a reaction to some event that has caused you to have an emotional response.

The majority of us have impulsive reactions to all sorts of situations. Example: let's say someone throws a basketball at you, you will try to catch it or you'll block your face from getting hit. That's an impulsive reaction, impulsive behavior is similar but different. Let's say a dude refers to your mother in a derogatory way and you immediately start punching him. That would be considered impulsive behavior. Another example would be, a car cuts you off on the road and you start cursing nonstop or try to run down the car to beat up the driver. That's also impulsive behavior.

For me, impulsive behavior is when someone says or does something that immediately enrages you into a violent outburst. I do believe this can be learned behavior. An example of how I've seen it taught is you are outside and you're joking around with some friends. One of your friends gets mad and calls you a disrespectful name or he says something about one of your parents. It made you mad but you just shake your head. The dude walks off and then one of your other friends say, "Man, I would have punched him in the face if he disrespected me or my mother like that." So, now you're telling yourself that the next time someone says something like that, you are going to punch them in the face. So, it happens again and you punched the person in the face. Then it happens another time and you remember to punch them in the face for disrespecting you. After a while, you stop remembering to punch them in the face because now it is your automatic response. Impulsive behavior. You become so alert that it may happen that you start swinging before anyone is able to get the whole word or phrase out. Now you're fighting all the time, getting suspended and locked up because someone disrespected you.

People who learn your triggers can start to use it for their amusement or to get you to fight their battles. Dudes may start telling you, "Man, so and so said, you're a punk, you ain't got no heart or your momma is this or your momma ain't that."

So, you're immediately enraged and you go and fight the person. You don't even investigate to see if the person actually said it or not. That may be partially because you trust the person who told you.

The reason I am mentioning this is so you can start re-evaluating your past reactions that led to you fighting. The more you learn about yourself, the more you can learn to change your responses. I suggest that you take a piece of paper and write at the top center, I'll fight you if you do this. Then draw a line down the middle and on the left side of the line write at the top what you will fight someone over. This list should consist of the things that you are willing to fight ANYBODY over! Don't just write "disrespect causes me to fight." You have to breakdown what is disrespectful to you. Example: If someone steps on my shoes, we're fighting. If someone calls me gay, we're fighting. If someone tries to hurt my friends, we're fighting, etc. Then on the other side of the page right down the consequences if you fight. Example: Violation of probation. Locked up. Mom mad at me again. He's going to try to kill me. I'ma have to really hurt him.

I want you to be able to identify what triggers you and the consequences. This could help you pause and not swing when it happens again. I'm not saying this will immediately change your responses but it can start to help you. These responses are learned behavior, so you can unlearn them if you want to gain control of yourself and stop getting in trouble. I want you to be able to recognize the real threats to your safety. Words may hurt your feelings, but you swinging or doing anything violent will lead to more serious issues for you. It doesn't make you less of a man if you walk away.

My goal is to help you stay out of trouble and be able to live a great life. You deserve it. You can have a great life, if you learn to better understand your life, and make decisions that will improve your life. You can do this.

Dudes Don't Take Me Serious

Does it ever feel like you always have to show dudes that you're not to be played with? Every time you go to a new school or move to a new neighborhood, you feel like you have to prove you're not soft or weak; that you're not a punk and you're not scared of anybody from around there.

I know you get tired of feeling that you have to prove yourself. It has happened too many times in the past, so now, when you start somewhere fresh, it's like you feel you have to make an example out of somebody. You just can't go anywhere new and just be you. Somebody is always testing you. It's crazy.

Then when a dude approaches you and you defend yourself, you're labeled a bully or troublemaker. Folks just don't understand that you are never the initiator. Plus, because nobody knows you, they're not going to step up and say that you didn't start it. Now the school or the cops are looking at you as the troublemaker because all of the trouble you have been in before. They're labeling you without knowing the full situation. I know you get frustrated. Then when you start telling your side of the story, they think you're talking back because you're speaking from frustration. Since nobody that saw the fight is going to step up and speak on your behalf, the administration may judge you based off of your school record. Translation: you'll get the blame. Now, you're in trouble again.

I know you hate this, but you expect it. It may have even reached the point where you want to just get it over with. It's simply the situation that new dudes are always put in. It may frustrate you that the administration may not recognize that this is the route for a lot of new or transferred students. You may feel the only benefit for you out of the whole situation, is that the people who you "needed" to know, now know that you're good with your hands so they leave you alone. However, there is an exception to that because now the knuckleheads want to become your friend. They want to hang around you. They start telling you how well you handled the situation and how much everybody will respect you now.

They now want to be associated with your toughness. They can use you to build or maintain their credibility. Some may even see you as their protector or they need you as a backup. I know you already know all of this if you have been through this before, if not, I wanted you to be aware. Know that most of them will never be a good friend to you. They'll keep you in trouble. Some of them will begin to act tougher than they are and turn to you when it's time to fight. Some of them will use you and leave you to suffer all the negative consequences.

I can't tell you how to choose your friends or how to end "the new dude experiences" but you have to trust your instincts. You have to listen to all conversations that take place around you. And with these new friends, if they are constantly talking about doing something that could get you in trouble, then **you've** allowed the wrong kind of people into your circle of friends.

Look, my advice isn't fool proof but you have to always recognize these kind of situations before they get to you. If you've had to prove yourself before, you know when the trouble is coming. You can feel it. You can see it in their body language, their eye-contact and from the instigators. But, you have to always remember there are consequences to your reactions, actions and the actions of those you closely associate yourself with. You have to remember every time you throw a punch, the cops, the security, the principal or somebody is coming for you and you're the one getting in trouble again.

You can resolve most situations by how you conduct yourself before it gets out of hand. It doesn't make you a coward because you don't want to fight. It makes you smart because you know some of the consequences if you fight: suspension, arrested, beat up or even killed. My advice is to avoid it as best as you can. You can do one of several things:

1. Leave the area when you sense that some drama is about to start. Don't wait to see if it is directed at you. You don't want to be involved either way.

2. When you know that you are about to be approached, don't go throwing your shirt, jacket, backpack or whatever on to the floor. That will instantly say that you want to fight. Instead stay calm and listen. When you respond, keep your voice as normal as possible. Look him in his eyes, not threatening but to be

assured you have his attention. Tell him or them that you don't want any problems. You're not looking for any trouble.

3. If you did something wrong, apologize.

4. Always stand out of range of being punched, or stand close enough not to be punched. Most of the time if two people are standing in each other's face, a fight is going to happen. So keep your distance and communicate that you don't want to fight.

5. If a group approaches you, step backwards where you can see everyone so you can't be sucker punched from behind and look for an escape route. There is nothing wrong with walking or running away to save your life. There is nothing about standing your ground, and getting beat up or possibly killed that makes you a man.

Haters

"A person that simply cannot be happy for another person's success. So rather than be happy they make a point of exposing a flaw in that person." - Urban Dictionary

Throughout your entire life there will be people who are going to judge you, underestimate you and see you for the first time and instantly not like you. They'll think you're not smart enough, you're not funny enough, you're a nerd, you're ugly, you're too handsome or your life is too easy. They're going to try to define you based off what they consider to be your flaws. The flaws that they will say you have are based off their imaginations, their experiences, people you remind them of, and what they have been taught to think about people who look like you. They may not even know you personally, nor do any of the things that they are saying about you have to be true. They just have to believe it to be true. So don't be surprised when you hear about people talking about you behind your back. They will tell people stories like you're poor or dirty because you don't wear the latest styles of clothing or because of the community that you live in. You'll have people saying things like, "You think you're better than everybody else" because you do wear the latest clothes and live in a better community. They may even dislike you because of the way you talk or how you walk. Just know that people will talk about you just because you are alive. Most people call them haters.

Now if you have already experienced this, eventually this will make you mad. Then you'll either convince yourself that you need to figure out how to get all of those material things, or if you have them, you will start denying that you do. I think this is a natural feeling because we all want to be liked and treated well. I just need you to understand that people gossip...all the time. They compare your life to theirs. Some will talk about you to try to impress other people who they want to be like or hangout with. Some talk because that's just what they do. Others try to direct everyone's focus on you so they won't be made fun of.

Now, I can tell you to ignore them, but that won't change how you feel. It won't make them go away. What I can tell you is that sometimes it is going to hurt. It's going to make you want to curse or even fight them. It'll hurt because someone is saying that something is wrong with you. It will make you doubt yourself and begin to wonder if they are right about you. You really have to do your best not to let them get into your head like that. If you do, you will find yourself making choices that you will regret. You can't allow their words to become your mirror.

Look, regardless of what you try to do to please them, you will never be able to make everybody happy or make everyone like you. It's not your responsibility to be everybody's friend or live up to their expectations. If you try to do that, you will start feeling like a failure. You'll find yourself hating the person looking back at you in the mirror because you're judging yourself with their eyes and not yours. The one thing you can't do is live your life based on what they believe you should be doing. This is your life.

Now, I won't lie. This is easier said than done. I realize this could be one of the biggest obstacles you'll have to get over again and again but you can do it every time. I just need you to understand that at the end of the day you have to live your life. Maybe at this exact moment you're not sure what you want to do with the rest of your life. I would suggest finishing school and staying away from negative people and situations that could get you in trouble. The beauty about school is that you are constantly learning about the world, how to solve problems and discovering what you're good at. Plus, no one can ever take away your education. Getting an education will not only help you to figure out what kind of career you want but it will help you to get it. However, you have to stay focused and don't allow anything or anyone to stop you from getting the education, It will help you be successful.

As far as your haters, let them hate. That's what they love to do. Who cares if they really don't like you. You can bet that they are always thinking about, talking about and watching you. They may really want to be just like you. Even if they want you to fail, that should empower and push you even more to succeed.

The last thing I want to say to you in this chapter, make sure you're not the hater. A few ways to check to see if you are the hater:

1. If you are always talking bad about somebody else, you might be a hater.

2. If you want someone to fail, you are probably a hater.

3. If you consider someone beneath you and you are constantly making them or other people feel less than, you have characteristics of being a hater. The cure is simple, stop talking about people and stop messing with people. In the end, you might get a few laughs but you will always be the joke. Because when you make fun or talk about other people, those same people are talking about you behind your back. They don't trust you. They know you're a hater and if you talk about other people, they wonder what you say about them. Being a hater is the easiest way to be the person no one likes.

Regardless of how you feel about your life right now, it won't remain the same. Whether it gets better or worse will depend on the decisions you make now. Don't allow haters to make you question what you are capable of. Just remember turning to the street life will not make your life better. It may seem like it because of the fast money but that money leads you straight to the grave or prison.

Stop Listening To Crazy People

I am sure you know someone who talks a lot of "let's go to war with the world" crazy nonsense all the time. They are always saying how they rebelled in the past. How they didn't allow the cops, the system, the establishment, the white man, the black man or any man or woman to get away with anything. They talk about how your generation is weak, soft or scared. They say how you have to fight back. They'll say you have to kill or be killed and how it's the only way to get respect. The thing I want you to always understand is that most of the time they are just venting or trying to get you mad enough to do whatever it is that they think that needs to be done. They'll always say, "It's the youngster's time to take over where us old timers left off," "Ya need to step up and stop accepting this stuff" or "What are you going to do?" They never include themselves in doing something other than running their mouth. If they do say that they are going to do something crazy, get away from them. You can try to calm them down, but these kind of people rarely calm down. They are always angry but for the most part, they are not going to do anything but talk about what they feel like doing.

However, they will try to convince you to jeopardize your life, your freedom and anything worth having. If they convince you to do it, you'll be dead or in jail and they will be telling the same stories to someone else.

Then there are those "crazy" folks, that tell dudes to quit everything, or attack everybody. I'm sure you've listened to their conversations when they're trying to tell dudes to quit school because it's a waste of time. They say, "why finish school when you're not going to have any money to pay for college?" or "you'll never find a **good job**." They're telling dudes that the white man is going to prevent you from being a success. The black or latino men are going to take your jobs. They're telling dudes to go to war with the police. They're telling folks to go to war with their friends and neighbors. They're telling dudes that a job is for suckers. They're basically telling you that nothing good can happen in your life unless you steal it, rob for it or go to war for it. I'm sure you've heard someone say at least one of those things to you or someone else.

If you haven't met these kind of people, trust me, you shall. They come in all shapes, sizes, races, jobs and businesses. They may not be "crazy" but they have lost hope in what they can accomplish with their lives so they try to spread their hopelessness on to you. Just know, you can accomplish anything you want. There are obstacles and people who will never like you. But those are challenges you can overcome. Don't allow these crazy talkers to shorten your life or your freedom by believing in them. Their failures don't belong to you or define you. Their present life isn't your future. They have made decisions or had life experiences that led them to the life they are living. You have more opportunities than they may have had. Take advantage of all the opportunities that can help you succeed and avoid the ones that will make you one of the "crazy" people.

Mad At Moms

It seems the closest person to us is our mom and we tend to take out our frustrations on her, our younger siblings, our communities and other people. But mom is usually the focus because we blame her if Dad is not there. We blame her for the things we can't afford. We blame her for not understanding us. We blame her for things we can't control. We blame her when we don't know who else to blame.

I know as young dudes we may not know how to express every need we have, but we expect her to know us better than we know ourselves. She gave us life, how could she not know we need her to solve a problem? How is it possible, she can't make it better? I know feeling like that made me angry, and I decided at 11 years old I was going to make my own life better. I was going to start taking care of me. Forget everybody else. I blamed my mother for everything that went wrong in my life. The thing that we miss is that she is the one who has never walked away.

We really don't understand how tirelessly she is working to keep the roof over our head, food in our bellies and give us what she can afford. We just know what we want. What's important to us and what is missing in our lives. It's us being selfish.

The thing is, she may be focused on the more important things that we need to live. The best life she can provide for us. If she is working all the time, you have to know she would prefer to be there with us at home. Someone has to work to pay the bills. It's hard on her especially if she is taking care of us by herself. If that is the case, there are going to be times when we feel she isn't doing enough. She isn't spending enough time with you. When you start feeling like that, I suggest that you sit with her and tell her how you feel. I assure you that she will do her best to solve that problem. Maybe you can suggest to her that the two of you have a special day every week to catch up on what's going on in your life, how you're feeling and what you would like from her. You should also tell her how you plan to make her day better. The one thing you can't do is say you are going to start making money committing crimes. This can never be any of your options.

Now if she is addicted to drugs or alcohol, I know how frustrating and embarrassing that is for you. I know it's a struggle not to lose all respect for her. You're confused at how she can make drugs and alcohol more important than her responsibilities to you. I know that pain and anger.

I don't know what caused your mom to start using drugs, but it isn't easy for her to stop if she is addicted. I know three ways people start using drugs.

1. Stress. Sometimes people become so overwhelmed and stressed with things like, trying to make their relationships work and paying their bills. They get tired and want to forget about their problems for a little while so they turn to drugs to try to escape.

2. Their friends convince them that being high before you go to a party makes your experience awesome. They tell them drugs like weed, is harmless. However, I believe weed can be addictive, because most people fall in love with it and want to be high every moment that they

are awake. And it has been known to lead to harder drug use and abuse.

3.   The person they are in a relationship with uses drugs and alcohol and encourages them to try it and they do.

I just want you to understand that it is extremely hard for people to quit using drugs if they are addicted to it. Even though you're angry, I want you to keep loving her. She isn't completely herself. The drugs are distracting and controlling her thoughts, her moods and her actions. You have to know that she loves you. I need you to do your best to watch over her and to make sure she is safe. I need you to keep encouraging her to quit. Remind her that she is better than what the drugs are turning her into. You have to let her know that you love and support her, and are willing to do whatever it takes, to help except supporting her drug habit. Don't you dare consider getting involved in the drug game to provide drugs to her. I know you want to keep her in the house. I know you don't want her sleeping with men for drugs and money. However, you selling drugs to support her habit doesn't help either of you. It will make your lives worse. The only thing you should do is seek out help for her from drug counselors, family members, etc.

I know sometimes you get angry and you want to scream at her. You want to fight her when she uses food money to buy drugs and you're left hungry. Just know that it is never right for you to raise your hands at her. You can't do that. I understand you feel like she is ruining your life. I know that anger, but you have to allow yourself to become calm before you talk to her. Shouting and screaming isn't going to help you, her, or the situation. You have to remind her that you need her and that there are programs like NA and AA that exist to help people struggling with a drug addiction to get clean.

When She Says, No

I am not sure if you are interested in dating. For you, this may even be a weird topic to have in this book, but I believe at some point in your life you will be very interested in dating. Dating may be the only thing you will be able to think of for a long time. So I need you to understand the biggest rule in dating that every man needs to respect.. If you don't respect this rule, you could lose your freedom or your life.

I know you have heard the saying, "No means No." It's true. If she says, "No", "Not now", "hold up," " I don't want to," "Stop," "That hurts," "Wait," "We shouldn't," "Let me think about it," "This is wrong," "I'm not in the mood," "I can't" or anything else she says other than Yes translates into NO. Yes is the only word that means she wants you to touch her, kiss her or even have sex with her. Any other word means she doesn't want to know you in that way.. You should instantly stop. If you don't stop, it can be considered harassment and if you physically try to touch her it can be considered RAPE and you can go to jail.

I don't care if she is laughing or smiling when she says STOP; you STOP. I don't care how many times you have had sex with her before. I don't care if she is your girlfriend. I don't care if she has slept with everybody else in your neighborhood. I don't care if she was naked and you all are having sex. When she says stop, you stop. It's rape if she doesn't give you permission to have sex with her. I don't care if she was high or drunk. If she uses any word, can't use words, can't move at all OR uses MOVEMENT that suggest she doesn't want to have sex with you-you stop.

This MOVEMENT also includes her using her hands to push you away, her crossing her legs so you can't enter her, her twisting her body away from you, her turning her head away from you and if she is about to cry or is crying, you stop. Those are only a few of the signs I can think of that mean that she does not want to have sex with you. If you don't stop, you can and will go to jail.

So far I covered the females you know personally or are dating. It is without a doubt a crime if you force or drug a female so you can have sex with her. Forcing a strange woman or a woman you know into a building, alley, forest, bushes, vehicle or anywhere else when she hasn't agreed to go with you, that is a crime. If you use a weapon and demand her to go somewhere or do something sexual to you, that is rape. Rape is a crime. If you decide you will get a woman drunk on liquor or high on drugs so you can have sex with her, that's rape. If you give a woman some kind of pill or "love" potion to make her horny or delusional so you can have sex with her, that's rape. If you see a female somewhere and you know she is drunk or high off a drug and you decide to have sex with her, that is rape. If she is asleep and you decide to have sex with her, that is rape. I don't care how sexy she is. I don't care if she is a prostitute. I don't care if you know you will never see her again. I don't care if she is high. I don't care if she is drunk and you think she won't remember. I don't care if she flirted with you before. I don't care how bad you think she wants it, forcing a woman to have sex with you is not right. It's wrong. It's a crime. Plus, her family may come after you to kill you and/or you will go to prison where you may be raped and murdered.

Now not only will you be disliked in your community for raping a female, there is a chance you will be raped and murdered in prison for having done that to a woman. You may have heard the stories that rapists of women and children are tortured in prison.

Just remember No means No.

Smoking Marijuana

Smoking weed seems to be the new popular thing. It's legal in some states. Everybody is doing it. It's supposed to have some health benefits and it is supposed to help keep you calm. That's what people say. So, if it is so good, why am I having this conversation with you? I figured you may be smoking it or you're curious. The only thing I can do is make you aware of some stuff. I'm sure you know weed is a drug? I'm sure you know it can be addictive. Well, most weed smokers say that they can stop whenever they want because they're not addicted to it. They just enjoy it. I just believe if you smoke something every day and several times a day, you're addicted. I believe if you steal weed from somebody, rob somebody for it or hang around people only because they may give you some of theirs, that sounds like an addict to me.

Most young dudes think addicts are people who are dirty, smelly, living on the street, have sores on their bodies and look like they are dying. It's true many addicts end up looking that way. But you can be an addict and don't look like that. I consider you a junkie or addict if you can't function without using the drug. If you're always thinking about it and trying to figure out how or where you can get some, you're addicted. The dictionary says an addict is: "a person who cannot stop doing or using something, especially something harmful."

I know a few everyday weed smokers. I have a program called, Passport To A New Life, where my team and I work with juveniles who are charged as adults. These kids are 14 to 17 years old and facing life in prison. The majority of them say that they smoked weed every day. They even said that they took (basically stole or robbed) weed from a friend or a stranger. They've told me they had to smoke a blunt[1] every morning, during the day and before they went to sleep. When I looked at their pictures when they first came to the jail, their hair wasn't cut, their lips were darker and they didn't look so clean. They all told me that they weren't junkies or addicted to the drug. They just loved getting high. They told me the only thing weed used to do to them was make them hungry or it relaxed them. I asked them were they high when they were arrested, the majority of them said, yes. So it seems smoking weed distorts their

---

[1] Blunts-weed inserted into empty cigars or wrapped in cigar paper and smoked

judgements. It made them do things they wouldn't do if they weren't high or it made them do things they wouldn't normally do to get high. It sounds like they were addicts to me, but they still didn't see themselves as that. I also asked them if they could smoke some weed right now would they, most said that they would. These kids are locked up facing all kinds of years in prison but they will violate the prison rules to smoke some weed; a drug that they're not addicted to. They sounded like addicts to me.

Oh, some of them said that they started using harder drugs like molly, snort powder cocaine, percocet, xanax, coricidin, ecstasy, klonopin, suboxone, hydrocodone, lean, nyquil, vicodin, tramadol, trazodone, mushrooms, oxycodone, oxycontin, superman, blue dolphin, glue, tobacco, wine, beer, bath salt and wax. All of them said that they started with weed but weed either stopped getting them high, they couldn't find any weed or they just wanted to try something new.

Many folks call marijuana or weed "the gateway drug." I've learned that it is the first drug that individuals begin smoking before trying harder drugs. Example: if you are smoking weed on a consistent basis and it stops getting you high, you try to find "better weed" but when you can't find weed strong enough to get you high, you try a harder drug like meth, angel dust, speed, cocaine or heroin.

If you still don't believe weed can make you an addict or junkie as the streets call them, let's look at it from another perspective. How about we look at it from a drug dealer's point of view and I used to be one. The dealer's goal is to make as much money as possible. The dealer isn't in the business to sell you the healthiest drug. Their goal is to have you come back again and again to spend your money on their drugs. They need you. They need your repeat business as soon and as often as possible. They need you to love them because you love what they are selling you. They want you to struggle to function without their drugs in your body. In other words, they need you addicted to their drugs. This means the first time you try their product, they have to make sure you have a mind-blowing experience. They have to make sure you get very high and feel good all over. It's the only way you will come back to look for them and their product. They need you desperately looking for them. They don't want to look for you. They need you to chase them...wherever they are...you'll get there because you want to feel that same high that you felt the first time or you want to feel even better than the first time. So, they have to keep providing you with the best products that they can find, or create the best drugs that they can make.

Every time you see them, they'll tell you or your friends that today's batch is better than the last batch. So if you thought the last batch of drugs you purchased was good, that means this batch will be awesome. Dealers always become greedy. The more money they make, the more they want to make. They're addicted too. They're addicted to the money and the lifestyle that you pay for.

If the dealer gets really greedy or the supply is low, they have been known to stretch their products by mixing it with some other chemical or drugs to make it more powerful or they sell you some fake drugs. Weed dealers have been known to sprinkle some meth, cocaine, heroin, angel dust, PCP or whatever on their weed to make you higher and to get you more addicted. In turn, this increases how many times you buy from them. The results on your end are that you start spending more money until you run out. After you run out of money, most addicts start trying to borrow money from people they know. Have you ever done this?

Once their friends stop loaning them money, they start trying to sell the dealer their belongings or they'll try to sell things to a pawn shop. Stuff like sneakers, jackets, TVs, video games, furniture, cars and anything that they own and believe someone will buy. Have you ever seen this?

Next, they may try to sell weed for someone to make a few dollars so they can always have it. The problem with that is, they begin smoking some of the product and not paying the money that they owe. Now the dealer beats them up or kills them. The addict may also try to sell some other kind of drugs for someone else with the same results.

Once they've sold everything that they own and fail as drug dealers, they have to find another way to try to get the money for drugs. You may start to see them outside of the gas station, at the bus stops, walking up and down the street asking you for money. They'll say something like, "Man, my car broke down." "I just came home from prison."

"I need 50 cent or a $1 to get on the bus." "Can you spare some change?" Have you ever seen them?

Some addicts may start stealing from family members and out of stores to sell the stolen goods to dealers. If that fails, they start trying to steal the drugs from the dealer's drug stashes. Which can cause them to be murdered.

Another thing addicts may do is rob unsuspecting people. They'll break in cars, snatch purses, knock people over the head, rob people with knives, bricks, guns or whatever they can get their hands on. They'll even try to rob you with fake guns and other fake weapons. Have you ever heard those stories in your community?

I've also seen weed smokers try to sell their bodies. Have you ever seen a woman on social media posting, "Who got that good good? Hit me up?," "I'm bored? Who can come through and put me in a cloud," "Ready to get my party on. Let's put it in the air. Who got it? Hit me up." or many other code words for I want to trade sex for weed. Have you ever seen those postings?

I know many people say weed would never be addictive or mess up someone's life. I ask you to think about the people you know who smoke weed every day. How often do they need it? How often do they talk about it?

Begin to look at yourself if you smoke weed. How often do you want it? How often do you think about it? Then look at your circle of friends. Are all of them just like you in terms of smoking weed? How often do some of them want it? Are some of them willing to steal it, sell stuff for it or sleep with someone for it? You may see it in your friends but not in yourself but look for changes in their behavior.

All drugs and liquor can be addictive. They all can cause you to stop focusing on your future, careers, school and all other things you care about. Most addicts become totally focused on getting and staying high. Most drug users who use cocaine, heroin and other drugs have said that they started with the "gateway drug" which is marijuana or weed before they tried other drugs.

I don't know when it became cool to get high. However, it seems that getting high is associated with being fun and exciting. There is nothing fun or cool about getting high. The only thing you get out of getting high is becoming dependent on the drugs that will turn you into a junkie. We both agree that junkies aren't cool. Junkies lose themselves and everything they ever had. Drugs keep them from ever owning or becoming anything but homeless and dying alone in the streets. I don't want that for you.

Lastly, if you don't believe weed is the "gateway drug," ask a junkie what was the first drug they used. If they say weed, then your research would have given you the same results as mine. So, don't take my word for it, ask a junkie and look at your friends to see how they have changed since smoking weed.

Keeping Your Word

Keeping your word is telling someone that you will do something specific for them and you do it. It's a verbal agreement like an unwritten contract. It's the reassurance that you will do something that you promised to do. When you do exactly what you said you were going to do, it shows people that they can depend on you. If you don't do what you promised, people will stop trusting you. The hardest thing to regain from someone is their trust.

However, there are some limitations to keeping your word. If keeping your word means you jeopardize your freedom, your safety, your life or someone else's life, then keeping your word is a fool's move. Good example: You tell me that you will pick me up at the airport at 4pm and drop me off at home. When you show up on time, that's keeping your word. Not keeping your word is if you tell me that you will pick me up from the airport, and you knew when you told me that you weren't going to pick me up. This would make me lose respect for you and I won't trust you when you say that you are going to do something. I'm going to see you as a liar. So you only agree to do something that you can and will do. It's better to tell people that you can't do something, than make them believe you can and will. If you can't do it, tell them. This will give them the opportunity to ask someone else to do it.

Lastly, you don't give your word to everybody. You only offer your word to do something you can deliver. You don't give your word to prove a point. You don't give your word on a dare. You don't give your word to commit a crime. You would be surprised how many people give their word that they will do something crazy, like punch someone in the face for someone or drive a getaway car for a bank robbery. Even if they really don't want to do it later on, they will honor giving their word. I can respect their commitment to living by their word, but I don't respect them giving their word to participate in a crime, where they can lose their life or end up in prison.

Again, don't give your word to something that is going to cause you or anyone else any harm.

Let's Talk about drug dealing

If you come to or live in the hood, you probably can look out of your window and see drugs being sold. You see the money exchanging hands so it looks easy. The sad part about anything illegal is that it is usually easy to do. You may be thinking about getting some drugs to sell to help your mom with a few bills, buy you some outfits or just to have a little money in your pocket. The problem is that it's going to take your whole life into a direction you really don't want to go. The other issue is you. If you live in a community where drugs are being sold you are already seeing the lives that it is ruining now. So for you to decide to start selling drugs, just know that you will be responsible for ruining other people's lives. You might be thinking that you can make you some quick cash and be done with it. What happens when that money runs out? I can tell you what happens, you will sell some more drugs to get you more money, because you will always need more money. But what if you sell drugs to someone who dies from the stuff you sold them? Now you may be facing a murder charge.

I'm sure you know someone or maybe even one of
your family members is an addict, and they use the
money that they are supposed to feed their kids
with to get high. Just think about how you could be
stopping another kid from eating. If you have little
siblings or cousins, imagine them being hungry
with no food to eat. You would do whatever you
could to feed them, but you're willing to hurt
another kid by selling their parent some drugs.
You might be saying, "If they don't get it from me,
they will get it from somebody else." That may be
true, but you are only responsible for your actions
and if you have ever been hungry and there was
no food to eat, you would understand how their kid
feels. If this still doesn't change your mind about
selling drugs then you're either desperate for
money or you're careless. If either of those is the
case, you can earn money another way. We'll get
to that in a few minutes. Keep reading.

Well, check this out, have you ever considered that
the same person who you sold the drugs to could
come back later with a weapon and kill you? Not
that you did something wrong or sold them bad
drugs, they're coming back to rob you to get the
rest of your drugs. They don't have any more

money, so the only way that they can get high is to take it. They decide it is better to kill and take the drugs instead of stealing the drugs and have you and your boys coming after them. It happens a lot. Have you even considered that while you're trying to make this fast money, the police are doing surveillance of the area? They see you and arrest you. Trust me, police not only do surveillances but they know the tricks of the drug trade. They know where people stash their drugs. They watch to see who hangs with whom. They stop you to learn your name and address. Don't you think for one minute that the cops are stupid. There are more people in jail for drug offenses than there are for anything else. Have you ever seen on the news or in newspapers how many people are in prison? There are almost three million people in prison in the USA. Most are not there because they turned themselves in. Just think about how many people in your neighborhood or in your family have been arrested or imprisoned. Most of that came from police investigations and surveillances.

Let's say you start selling drugs and you get arrested. Now you have a criminal record that may prevent you from getting in certain schools or that job you want to get after you graduate from school. Getting locked up can ruin your opportunities to accomplish many things you want in the future. Have you ever heard anybody in your life complain about not being able to get a good job because of their records? That means that they have been arrested and or convicted of a crime. So, when the company that wants to hire them looks up their social security number, they find that they have been arrested or convicted of a crime. That kills the opportunity to work for that company because many companies have policies that don't allow them to hire individuals with criminal records.

Did you know that getting locked up for selling drugs can get your whole family evicted? If you are arrested in your complex for selling drugs, you can get your family put out by the rental office. So your decision doesn't just affect you. It can make your family homeless. Your mother and your siblings living on the street all because you wanted to sell drugs. Did you also know if the police arrest you and get a warrant to search your house and they find drugs, they can arrest your mother and everyone else in the house? Again, you will be the cause of your family becoming homeless and possibly arrested.

Do you know that every year over 3,000 kids are murdered because of their involvement with drugs and crime? Did you know that every year thousands of kids are sent to juve[2] and adult prisons because of getting involved with drug dealing and crime? They all were trying to make some fast money. They thought they could do it and get away with it. Now they are dead or in jail. Just think about that for a second. How many of your friends are in juve or have been in juve or are in prison? How many of your family members are there?

I am sure if you are considering selling drugs, you know at least two people who are doing it now. How often do they think or talk about the police? Do they always seem nervous or watching their back? How many times have they been arrested? How many people told you to stay away from them? Your mom or whomever are warning you to stay away from them because they know that

---

[2] "Juve" is a abbreviated term for the juvenile system.

sooner or later those people are going to jail, getting shot or killed from selling drugs.

It seems cool and easy but trust me, it's not. There may be an older guy or woman who is telling you how easy it is, because they want you to sell drugs for them. Let me tell you something, they are trying to put you on flunky time. They want you to sell drugs for them so they don't put themselves in jeopardy to get locked up or get shot. See, they want you taking all of the risk, you making all of the money and then turning it over to them. How many people your age that you know have been killed or have court cases? How many are locked up now? I know I keep mixing jail or being killed into this conversation. Murder and prison go together with crime. Eventually if you are involved in doing crime one of those things is going to happen to you. Guaranteed.

If you're not thinking of selling drugs but your friends are drug dealers, let me let you in on something else. If you hang with drug dealers or people breaking the law and the police do a drug bust, they will more than likely lock you up too. I know I mentioned surveillance earlier but I want to make sure you get this. The cops are watching when you may not see them. They write down who the dealers are hanging with and they take pictures of you all together. So when they arrest them, they may be arresting you for conspiracy. That simply means that you planned and plotted to sell drugs with them. The other thing that you may not be aware of is if the person they are selling drugs for have dealers in other parts of the city or the country and they have killed someone, it's included in the conspiracy charge. You may be innocent but you'll have to prove it in court. The prosecutors will show surveillance photos of you hanging with the dealers on multiple occasions. They'll make it look and sound like you knowingly participated in the criminal enterprise. Then when they show the jury the pictures of the dead bodies, they will point to you. They will say, "these men conspired to kill this person or these people and they didn't stop until they killed them." When you have a chance google "The RICO Act" and read what it tells you about how prosecutors take down drug and other crime rings. Most of my childhood friends are doing life in prison for conspiracies and many of them were just seen or hanging with drug dealers.

Here is something else I want you to think about if you're hanging with drug dealers. Let's say you are hanging outside at a school, in front of your house, by the corner store or even in a car, and the police speed up, jump out of their cars and place you all on the wall. Or let's say that they pull over a car that you're a passenger in and they find drugs in the car, they will lock everyone up. How many of your drug dealer friends are going to say that the drugs are theirs? If they were going to claim the drugs, chances are they wouldn't have thrown them or hidden them. Most of the time drug dealers throw the drugs and run off but you don't run because you're not guilty. Who do you think the police are going to lock up when they find the drugs? Yeah, you.

Let's say you are friends with drug dealers but you don't hang with them but you all are cool because everybody lives in the same area. They may be recruiting you to sell drugs and you might not be aware of it. However, I will make you aware how this works. Has a drug dealer ever asked you to warn them by making some kind of noise if you see the police coming? For doing just that, you can be charged with conspiracy to distribute drugs. Has a drug dealer ever pointed to their hidden drugs and told you to keep an eye on it for them until they come back? Even if you don't touch it, you are still conspiring and can be arrested. Has a drug dealer ever asked you to hold their drugs for them until they get back? What will happen if the police stop you and find those drugs? Who will they arrest? Even if you tell them those are not your drugs, you are in possession of them. You will be arrested for possession of an illegal controlled substance and depending on the amount of drugs, you can be charged with the more serious crime of distribution. Has a drug dealer ever asked you to hold some drugs for them until they get back but then they tell you how much each piece of drugs are worth? Then they say, if someone asks for one just give them one and make sure you take this amount of money from them? Who you think the addict is going to tell sold the drugs to them if the police stops them? You. Who do you think the police will have a picture of selling the drugs? Yeah, You. See you were being recruited to sell drugs and you thought you were just looking out for a friend. Drug dealing is full of people who are willing to put your life on the line and walk away like they have never seen you before. Most drug dealers are killed by their best drug dealer friends.

Let's say the drug dealer showed you where their drugs were hidden and asked you to watch that area for them but you leave and come back and someone else stole the drugs, what do you think the drug dealer is going to say or do to you?

1. The dealer tells you that it is cool and don't worry about it?

That will never happen! The dealer will be pissed because not only did they lose product, they lost money.

2. He will tell you that you owe him or her the money for the drugs?

If you don't have the money, you will probably have the option to sell their remaining drugs to repay the debt.

3. That damages the relationship you had with the dealer. The dealer asks you to do something foolish to repay the debt?

I remember a dealer made this guy that lost his drugs to go snatch a ring out of a jewelry store to repay the debt.

4. Ask you to arrange for him to sleep with a woman in your family like your sister?

5. The dealer thinks you're lying and beats you up?

Depending on the amount of drugs, you could be killed.

You thought this was your friend. There are no friends in the drug game or any other crime. You are only a tool to help them make or keep their money.

What I hope you will remember if you don't remember anything else, every decision that you make has a consequence. I made you aware of the potential negative outcomes to becoming a drug dealer. To be honest, there are no positive outcomes unless you choose not to get involved at all.

GANGS

I know we need to have a conversation about
gangs. I don't know how you feel when you hear
the word gang, when you see a gang or if you are a
part of one. I just want to make sure I can tell you
what I know about them. You and I are supposed to
keep each other on point. Right? So I'm going to
tell you what I know about gangs and the kind of
people who generally get involved with them. I
have only been around gangs, crews, mafia, posse,
and cartel members. Be mindful my interaction
with these guys were in prisons with higher
ranking members and leaders. However, I have
dealt with posse and crews more in communities.
First of all, the names are different but they are
basically the same: a group of friends who commit
crimes in certain communities. The only exception
is crews. My experience with crews is that they
tend to be people who live in the same community.
They are usually individuals who know each other
but don't normally sell drugs or commit crimes as
a team. Some of them do sell drugs and commit
crimes together but they don't have rules
specifying that you can never get out. For the
most part, they come together if someone else

comes into their community and starts trouble or kills someone they know. Then they may join forces and retaliate together. However, they usually just hang together at parties and clubs. They do identify their neighborhood as where they are from as a form of status. That is the difference between crews, gangs, mafia and posses. The other groups usually have rules that dictate how members are initiated, how they dress, operate and commit crimes. They operate as a whole and not as independents. They also have someone who is considered the leader.

I believe there are four kinds of people who join gangs: individuals that are forced into the gang, individuals who want to prove they are tough, individuals who want to feel they are a part of a family and individuals who want to be protected.

Answer this for me. Do you feel your family isn't taking care of you or loving you the way that you need? Do you argue with your parents a lot and have run away a few times? Do your parent/s use drugs and spend the money on drugs instead of taking care of you? Does your parent pay more attention to his or her boyfriend or girlfriend than they pay to you? If you said yes to any of those, you probably feel lonely and alone. Chances are you prefer to spend more time with your friends than around your family. Plus, some of your friends are experiencing the same issues at home that you are experiencing so you all have that in common. They understand you, right?

If you feel unloved at home, you may find gangs more interesting because many of the gang members you know have the same problems that you do. If you are a runaway, you know other runaways. When you run away you probably are hanging out with other runaways all night in the streets. You all sleep in parks together, you all sleep behind buildings together and you all have shared your food with one another. Sometimes you may steal the food. Chances are if you run away more than one time, you have spent sometime in the juvenile system where you met other runaways and gang members that you became friends with.

I just know through these relationships you find more kids that are considered troubled, bad, or at-risk kids. You all start to stick together. Some of those kids that you meet will have parents who may allow you to stay over their house for a night, few days or move in with them.

More established gangs are very inviting to run away and troubled kids because they offer food and shelter. They usually have homes you can sleep in. They even seem to control vacant buildings, vacant homes and vacant storefronts that you can sleep in. Many of those place are used to sell drugs out of, but you don't pay that any attention because you just want to sleep there instead of in the streets. They'll make sure no one bothers you. If someone bothers you, they are bothering them so you all fight together. This is the kind of love and support you were looking for. This feels like what a family should feel like. So you tell yourself that these are my boys. This is my family. We ride and die together. It feels comfortable. They understand and love you, right?

You all sneak onto the subway and buses together to get around town. It's funny. You all laugh about those experiences. You have a good time with them. Then the group gets hungry and nobody has any money. So they ask you to steal out of the store this time. You really don't want to do it but you look at your boys and they look hungry. This is your family. They have stolen before to feed you so you can do it this time. You have convinced yourself. You do it and get away with it. You all laugh about it. It was easy so you keep doing it.

Then someone in the group says that you all can get more money if you all snatch a purses. It happens. You get away with it. You all laugh about how scared you were, how the woman reacted and how fast the group ran. It was funny, right? Then the drug house where you sleep tells you that you can't stay there anymore unless you help them make money. You look around at your friends and some of them have already been selling drugs. You start telling yourself, If they can do it, you can do it. This is for the family. You all need to continue to sleep here. It's cold or too hot or too dangerous to start sleeping back outside. So now you're selling drugs for the gang. Then one of the gang members gets killed. You are angry. Your friends are angry. Then the gang leader brings some guns and say, "we have to avenge our fallen soldier's death." You don't want to, but they killed one of your brothers. The leader passes around some drugs to take away some of the fear. You all use the drugs. You go out and the gang gets revenge. How did your family who loves you turn you into a group of thieves and murderers? All you wanted was to be understood and loved. Then the leader tells everyone never to talk about it or they will kill you.

Gangs have that appearance of a loving family. A lot of gang members are runaway teens and teens who have been put out by their parents. They appear to support you in everything you do. They have your back all the time. The only problem is that gangs don't support you living a good life. So, teens who don't get along with their families seem to join gangs because they provide places to sleep or they become a family to those who don't have a family at all. Gangs can provide a sense of false security and belonging to their members.

One of the things you need to understand about gangs is that everyone isn't there to feel loved. Many gang leaders see this as a way to build their reputation and build their wealth. So gangs become violent whether that was their initial goal or not.

There are a few other things I want you to understand about gangs. You have no freedom to do what you want. If the gang leader tells you to kill someone, beat someone up, shoot someone or even sell drugs, you have to do it. If you don't do it, you can be killed. You can't even refuse to use drugs if you don't want to. They will say you are not loyal or you may be a snitch if you don't do what the leaders tell you to do.

Another thing about gangs, they try to convince you that the community you live in is yours to protect. This means you are not allowed to just let outsiders come in your community and sell drugs, commit crimes or even just move in the area. Just think about this. How many gang members that you know of are not destroying their community? Do they throw trash around? Do they spray paint gang signs and names on the walls? Don't they sell drugs to people who live in the community? Don't they rob people in their community? Don't they intimidate people in their community? So how are you protecting a community if you are doing things to make the community a bad place for the people who live in them?

Again, gangs become violent whether they intend to or not. Just think of the gang members you know. Who are they at war with? Why are they even at war with them? A lot of older gangs are at war with other gangs because someone was killed 20 years ago or because they wore a different color bandana, or were a different race than each other. Do you really want to become a gang member, and go to war with someone else, because they don't wear the same color of clothing that you do? Do you also realize that this means you can never wear any color of clothing that other gangs wear? I just want you to think about this and tell me do you want to live like that?

Being a part of a gang also makes you responsible for retaliating against anyone who shoots someone or kills someone from your gang. How many gang members do you know who are now dead? Why did they get killed? Was whatever they did or did not do worth them losing their life? So many gang members are being killed now, because they were walking down the street, and their rival gang members see them wearing the wrong colors. Do you really want to live this way? Once you get in, you're in until you're dead. You can't even escape if and when you go to prison. The thing I want you to think about is that you are told what to do. You are not allowed to refuse. You can tell your mother no at times but you can never tell the gang no. If they tell you to kill someone in front of his child or even the police, you have to do it or risk getting hurt badly or even killed.

If you are one of those individuals who wants to prove you're just as tough as any other boy, you don't have to join a gang to prove that point. The best way to prove this to yourself and anyone else is not to join a gang. Being able to beat someone up or kill someone will never make you a man. It may make people scared of you until someone else who wants to show how tough they are and kills you to prove they are tougher than you. Another scenario is that some gang leaders may see you as a threat to their power and have you killed if they believe you have more influence or more people in the gang are scared of you than they are of them. Or another gang that you are at war with will see you as the main person they have to kill to weaken your gang. You can't build a reputation without telling people or showing them what you did. This will lead to the police looking for you to arrest you. The other side of that is that the police will consider you armed and dangerous and any false movement on your part can get you shot and killed.

Fear never equals respect. Fear equals people hoping something really bad happens to you so they can stop being scared of you. I know you have heard the saying, " a scared person will kill you quick because they are so afraid that you will kill them." It's true. Again, fear doesn't equal respect and it sure doesn't mean you are a man because people are scared of you. There is always someone "badder" or more driven to prove they are "badder" than you and who will always target you. That's what fear does, it makes you a target for others to try to hurt and kill you.

If you are one of those individuals that gang members keep threatening or beating up to make you join the gang, my advice is to find someone in your community who the gang leaders respect. See if this person would speak to the gang leaders on your behalf to inform them that you don't want to be a part of the gang. Why this can work is because the gang leaders have a relationship with this person and they are more inclined to leave you alone because you all have a mutual respect for the same person. It won't hurt to ask several people you know who have a good relationship with the gang leader. Even if you know his girlfriend, she may be able to convince the leaders to leave you alone. Or if you know other higher ranking gang members, ask them to do it for you.

So, to avoid all of the pitfalls and consequences of gang life, never get involved with one. It will make your life worse than you currently believe it is now.

CATCHING "JUVE" CHARGES

One of the scariest things I have ever experienced was going to court on a new charge. I remember sitting there nervous because I didn't know what they were going to do with me. I felt powerless. I looked around and these people didn't even know me but they were going to decide what was going to happen with my life. I couldn't focus. I wanted to just leave. They started talking and I didn't even understand most of the words that they were using. From time to time the prosecutor would threateningly point at me with a look of disgust. I would ask my lawyer questions about some of the statements they were making about me. He basically would tell me to shut up. The judge would make me stand and ask me questions that I didn't understand or didn't know how to answer. All of this was strange and scary. Then something would happen where they would dismiss the case or release me to my mother's custody. My lawyer would have a brief conversation with us. He would basically tell me not to get rearrested and to get back into school. I used to be sincere in my response that I would do both. Then I would smile walking out of that courtroom feeling victorious.

As soon as I reached my neighborhood and one of my buddies would ask me "how did it go?" I would say, "I beat that case or I'ma beat that joint." So, we're celebrating my victory. I convinced them and myself that I beat the case. That the courts couldn't touch me because I was invincible. I didn't mention that I had no clue as to why the case was nolle prossed[3]. I acted like it was all my doing. Soon I went right back to hustling or whatever I was doing before I got caught. A few weeks later or a few months later I was back in court with a new charge. It seemed like the process repeated all over again. The case was thrown out of court. Now I'm back in my neighborhood and back to breaking the law again. I started to believe I was the luckiest or smartest dude in the street game. I started to believe in the lies I was telling my friends. Every time my case was nolle prossed/ thrown out/dismissed, I became more daring. I was convinced I could out smart any and every one. Have you ever experienced that or do you know somebody like that?

---

[3] The charge was **Nolle Prossed** or Dismissed.

This is how we trick ourselves. This is how we get setup. Every time our case is nolle prossed we take it as a victory. We tell everyone that we beat the case. We keep breaking the law. We go from stealing small stuff to stealing cars to selling drugs to firing guns. We keep catching new cases. We're the new criminals. The police in our community know us by our birth name and street names because they have stopped or arrested us so many times. We brag about the attention. We think we're respected and that the cops aren't smart enough to really make their case stick. However, the judges know we'll be back. The cops know we'll be back. Our parents even know we'll be back. We even know that we will be back because we haven't stopped breaking the law. We keep catching cases. The thing that we underestimate is that every case we ever caught will come back to hurt us. Then we catch that serious case. The judge looks at all those cases we caught before and decide to charge us as adults. It gets real to us real fast. Now we are facing 10, 20, 50 years or life in prison. No more 6 month or juvenile life. We're with the big boys.

Now we want to be given a second chance but it's a little too late. We tell ourselves, the lawyers, the judges and anyone else that "all we knew was the street life." The streets were the only way we knew how to survive. Life is hard. We were just trying to take care of our family. For the most part, you and I know that most of us were never trying to take care of our families. We were trying to take care of ourselves. Now, the streets may be all that we knew but it is/was all that we wanted. We think or thought that everything else takes too long or it doesn't earn us respect.

I do understand that if you are failing in school, or you're forced to take care of yourself, you feel limited in what you can do with your life if you are under 18. I understand that it is scary and maybe depressing and you don't know where else to turn. It seems the streets are the only place you can get what you need. I know it feels like your options are so limited that you believe you will be dead before you turn 18 or locked up for the rest of your life. I don't have all the answers. I just know if you are hustling or breaking any law, you are increasing the chances of you being killed or going to jail for the rest of your life.

Hopefully you are reading this book and see it as your wake up call. I hope you see this as your chance to change your life. Changing your behavior isn't going to be easy. However, you can do it. You may have to do some things you don't really want to do, or wait longer to get money or the kind of results you want today. I can guarantee you this, if you stop breaking the law, your chances of dying before 18 decreases drastically. Your chances of going to prison decreases drastically. The good thing is you can still get the kind of things you want out of life without putting yourself in handcuffs.

If you're homeless, I know it is hard living in the streets. I know you are already doing stuff you don't want to do. I know this may not sound like a good option but if you're homeless, go to a child protective agency. I know you don't want to live in foster care, but you'll have a bed, you'll be more comfortable than living in the streets during cold winters or hot summers. You will eat every day. You'll get to focus on school and your health. You'll find your way to success. If you have a family member that is willing to allow you to live with them, call them. I know you hate following their rules but their rules are not to harm you. It is to make you responsible, keep you safe and to make sure you have a chance at a great future. The rules of the street that you abide by now are going to kill you. If you keep catching cases, you will end up in prison. Trust me, I ended up there.

I'm just trying to get you to understand that someone does care about you. I know deep down inside you do care about yourself so do the right thing for yourself. You know what it is. You know choosing the streets leaves you with only these options: jail, death, paralyzed or shot up. Today you can start living your life differently. You can still make money. You just have to change your hustle to a legit one.

Reputations

If you are already in the street life and have built a vicious and violent reputation, you may feel that locks you into the game for life. I don't agree with that. I want you to consider a few options:

1. If your name strikes terror in your enemies because of the violence that you have been involved in, you do have a huge obstacle. I want you to think, how many of these people actually know what you look like? Sometimes we have a reputation and most of the people who are scared of us have never even seen us. They wouldn't even recognize us if we asked them for directions. Someone would have to point you out to them, for them to recognize you. That's one of the mysteries of having a reputation. Others have told boogeyman stories about you and that's what they fear. I have been in the presence of a few dudes telling a story about me and they didn't even know that I was sitting right there. What's crazy is, the story they were telling, wasn't true. I didn't even know anything about that incident. No, I didn't reveal myself to them. I didn't see the

purpose of adding a face to the name they feared. They spoke as if we were close friends. I had never seen these guys in my life.

Anyway, my point for telling you this story is because it taught me that if you stop using your nickname, the people who have only heard of you will never know that it is you. You really have to be committed to being out of the street life. I know it took you awhile to build that respect and name recognition. I just need you to know, that you're worth more than being a negative living street legend. Staying attached to that name will lead to your early death. Then you will be a dead legend. If you want to change your life, you have to discard your street reputation.

2. If your reputation is associated with your birth name, it seems harder to discard your name. Let's say that your name is Joe Smith and that's the name everybody knows. I suggest you stop using your whole name. Start introducing yourself as Joe or Mr. Smith. You should only use your whole name when you have to and not when you are

introducing yourself to people you don't know.

You will also have to ask your friends, family and associates to start calling you by your first name or your last name only. It will take some time for them and you, to get used to referring to you that way, but you can do it. You have to do it if you want to move away from your reputation.

3. If you have too many enemies that do recognize you when they see you, you will have to move with a relative out of town for maybe 2 years. It could be longer. To be honest, most dudes with violent reputations will not live or be free longer than 2 or 3 years. It may be harsh for me to say but you have to wait until they die off or go to prison.

There may be some that live past the expiration date I mentioned. You will know, because your friends and family will know that they are still alive. Most of them that live past a few years may have changed just like you have. If they have changed, they don't want to go backwards and wage war against you.

Now, what I am saying isn't guaranteed. I am just going by my experiences and the people I know who have violent reputations. The majority of them are dead. Most of those who are alive are in prison with 40 years to life sentences. There are the few who have given up on that life. I don't know anyone from my past that is still building their violent reputation.

Again, my goal is to help you find peace and a new life for yourself. You may never feel safe in your hometown and decide to stay in a new state. I just know, it is your way to have a chance to get away from the drama of this life you are living, and have a chance to do something different.

The biggest mistake you can make is moving out of town, and doing what you are doing in your current hometown. So, you have to be sure you really want a better life for yourself. You have to be honest with yourself, if you're not tired of the street life or you don't want to give up your reputation, then you will suffer the consequences of your choices. No one is invincible. Sooner or

later we all meet the person that is more vicious
and better at creeping than we are.

How to deal with the cops

If you live in an inner city, more than likely you have already been stopped, questioned and searched by the police. If you are a boy of color, chances are you have been stopped, questioned and searched several times by the police. It is believed there are a lot of reasons for this. It could be your race, you are a male and you live in poor communities where a lot of crimes are committed. These communities just happen to be where a high percentage of boys and men of color live.

However, I want your interactions with the police to begin and end well. I can't tell you how they are going to act towards you. I just want to help you to react in the best manner that will get you home.

It seems society says that males as a whole commit more crimes, but men of color are more likely to commit more crimes than any other race of men. I don't believe that. However, because that belief is out there you will automatically be a potential suspect to the police. Some believe if you haven't already committed a crime, you are in the process of committing one. Here are my suggestions when the police are approaching you.

1. Do your best to stay calm. I know it gets irritating because it seems they keep targeting you when you haven't done anything wrong. Stay calm anyway. Don't start cussing them out or talking back.

2. Don't run. If you aren't guilty of a crime, you shouldn't run. Even if you live in a state where they have "stop and frisk" and you have been frisked three times this month, don't run. I know it's annoying but running is only going to make them chase you. If they catch you, they will rough you up and probably lock you up.

3. You should always keep your school ID or driver's license on you. They'll ask for it. By having your ID, it should make your time with them shorter. They will run your name through the police system to see if you have any warrants.

4. When it comes back that you don't have any warrants, they may ask you a series of questions like, "Where you live." Even if that information is on your ID just answer the question.

5. They may ask you where are you going? Tell them.

6. They may ask if you have any drugs or weapons on you, just answer the question. Then they may ask if they can search you. You have a legal right to say no. My concern is that I don't want this to escalate into a confrontation. If you're not carrying anything and you say no, make sure you remain calm. Don"t start arguing and try to best to not pull away if they provoke you by touching you. If you do, they may say you were resisting arrest after they rough you up. My goal is to get you away from them as soon as possible.

7. They may ask you if you know anything about a crime that was committed around the area. Just tell them no. The goal here is for you to get home.

If you don't carry an ID, they can detain you until they verify who you say you are and you're not wanted for a crime. If they ask you where you live and you respond, " It's on my ID". They may take that as you being "disrespectful" and that could lead to them roughing you up or trying to provoke you to say or do something that can get you arrested. Just answer the questions as fast as possible so you can go on with your life. Don't be bothered if they write your name down in their notebook. It's their way of remembering your name or keeping a record of your name just in case it is involved in a crime. Them having your name isn't an issue if you're not getting into trouble. Now if you are committing or going to commit a crime and your name comes up and they look at their notepad, it will have your address on it.

In some areas they take pictures of people. I'm really not in agreement with them taking your picture if you're not under arrest. I'm also not in agreement with you consenting for them to take your fingerprints. They have no reason to take your fingerprints or picture if you're not under arrest. If they ask, just simply say, "Officer, I didn't do anything wrong so I'm not consenting to my picture or my fingerprints being taken." Then you can ask them are you under arrest. If they say no, ask them if you are free to leave. If they say yes, leave immediately.

Here are some things you should never do when you are being approached by the police:

1. Snatch or pull anything out of any of your pockets! Never do that! Don't dig in your pockets for your ID, cellphone or ANYTHING. You wait for them to tell you to retrieve your ID.

2. Never gesture with any object in your hand toward them. I don't care how harmless it is. They may think it is a weapon and shoot you.

3. If they approach you from behind, just pause. Don't turn around to face them until they tell you to do so. If you have a cell phone in your hand and your back is turned from their sight, let them know with your words that you have a cellphone in your hand. Don't turn around to show them because they may mistake it for a gun and shoot you.

4. Now if you are with someone and the police approach you, and the person you are with runs off, DON'T RUN. You just put your hands on

the nearest fence, wall, car or anything large and do not move. Hopefully, they will see you are not a threat and things will go well for you.

Furthermore, if you are driving or you are a passenger in a car and the cops pull the car over, you should place your hands on the dashboard, steering wheel or out of the window. Have your palms open so they can see that there isn't anything in your hands. Whatever you do don't start looking in the glove compartment, console, ash-tray, between the seats or in your pockets. The cops may get scared and think you are reaching for a weapon and kill you.

If you are the driver of a car and the police pull you over, cut the car off. Don't wind down the window until they ask you to. When asked, do so, with one of your hands still visible for them to see. You can ask them why they pulled you over. You can do that. Don't dispute anything with them. When they ask for your driver's license and registration, tell them where it is stored. Let them give you permission to reach for it. If they ask if they can search your car, you can say no.

They shouldn't ask you to step out of the car if you haven't committed a crime. A traffic stop isn't enough for them to ask you to exit the vehicle but they seem to always ask teenage boys to exit the car. You can ask them are you under arrest for something. You can also ask them why are they requesting you to exit your car. If they say, so they can search the car, you can tell them that you are not consenting to a search of the car. If they still demand you to get out of the car, do it. I don't want it to escalate into you getting arrested or hurt.

Try to get a good look at the officer's name and badge number. You can always tell your guardian what happened and they can file a complaint. If you can't read the name or badge, kindly ask them for it or try to remember the number on the police car. The police precinct should be able to track down the officer by the car number, the day you were stopped and an estimation of the time you were stopped. The goal is to not get into an argument with the cops. The goal here is to make sure you get home safe.

Sagging Pants

I know people have been telling you how disrespectful it is to have your pants sagging off your behind. They've told you it is a style that was created by homosexuals in prison. I'm not going to tell you to pull your pants up. I just want to make sure you're aware of something that you may have not considered. If this doesn't help, then do your thing.

First, let me tell you that I'm not positive that sagging pants started in prison. I was there for a long time. Nobody had their pants sagging. If they did, they would be raped. I believe sagging pants originated during slavery times when older folks gave their clothes to smaller children. The children used to tie a string, a rope or whatever they could around the waist of the pants to keep them from falling off. However, some of the clothing was so big that they still sagged.

Let me ask you a question:

What do you do or say when you see a female with a nice body? Do you be like, Dammmmmmmmmn!

She is thick? She has a dream body? I like that. I want that.

Does that sound like you? Ok. Now I want you to consider this. Let's say you and 10 of your boys are hanging out. All of you wear sagging pants. Imagine that you're walking pass one of your buddies and he looks at you as you're walking away. His focus is on your butt. He thinks to himself, "Damn, Homie is phat as hell."

How would you feel about that? You would probably want to fight him if you knew what he was thinking, right? However, you don't know what he is thinking. Nor do you know what all the other men and boys are thinking when you walk by with your pants sagging. Chances are some of them are thinking about you the same way you think about that female with the amazing booty.

I just wanted to give you something to think about.

Tattoos

Tattoos are extremely popular these days. I see young people and even grandmothers starting to get tattoos. You may have one or are considering getting one. I just want you to be cautious of where you put them and what kind you get. My suggestion is NEVER get a tattoo on your face, your neck or your hands.

I know that a lot of gang leaders require their members to get tattoos that will always be visible to the public. They call it "repping" your set. Usually the more visible your tattoo is the more committed you are to your gang. This may be why many gang members have tattoos on their faces. Other popular places are hands and necks. Sometimes I wonder if this is used to limit the gang member's opportunities to leave the gang. The majority of companies will never hire someone with a tattoo on their faces. You may never be able to find a high end job that's paying you tons of money if you have a tattoo on your face. You could never join the military if your tattoos are visible. My nephew had to get his removed from his face and hands to even be considered for the military.

Ok, you're a musician or some kind of artist and this is how you want to express yourself. Ok. I get it. You're very committed to your craft and self expression and it's your choice. However, I would just advise you to wait until you have a major record deal or you are making a lot of money and hits as an independent artist. I would discourage you from getting tattoos that will always be visible before you have your first hit, start touring, sign to a recording or distribution deal. You don't have to be tatted up to be perceived as street smart or hardcore" I know a lot of popular artists have tats on their faces. However, those tats didn't make them famous. Creating great art will do more for your brand than having tattoos. Look at Jay-z and 50 cents. They don't have tattoos on their faces, but they are both perceived as street dudes. I am not hating or discouraging you from capturing your dream. I believe you can make it if you stay determined, make great art and stay committed to not only making your art but selling it. I am just asking you to wait until the money starts rolling in. I'm only saying this because you may have to get a non-entertainment related job to fund your career. Again, regular companies seem to shy away from individuals with visible tattoos. This is because tattoos are usually associated with gangs and other outlaws and they don't want to give customers that impression.

If you ever get a tattoo, I don't suggest you get that exhibits hatred tattoo. You may be a part of a hate group today but you change later on in life and the tattoo is always visible and the kind of people you used to hate, will still see the tattoo on you. They will hate you or may even harm you. So, it's a safety issue as well. It can also be a health issue. It is a fact that some people have contracted diseases like HIV because the tattoo artist didn't clean the needles properly.

I want you to picture yourself in 10 years with a family. You have little kids that will be looking up to you. They will think every choice you make in life is good and they will make the same choices.. So before you get the tattoos on your face, hands and neck, envision your future young son's or daughter's eyes. Imagine your child is scared of the dragon, or other horrifying images that you have tatted on your chest. Every time you go to pick your kid up, they're scared of you because they're really scared of the tattoo. Or your son sees the gun tattoo on your body and thinks guns are cool, and wants to get one. He wants to be like you. He thinks if you like guns enough to get a tattoo, he can own a gun.

I know that may sound extreme but it is really possible because you will be one of your child's superheroes. I'm telling you this because we end up regretting a lot of the decisions we made as a teen.

This is the last thing that I will say about tattoos. Removing tattoos in general is expensive and painful. I strongly suggest that you never get a tattoo with someone else's name on you, like a female you are dating. If the two of you breakup, then you have to walk around with her name tattooed on your body. It will make your new girlfriend mad every time she reads your ex's name on her man's body. Now you have to cover the tattoo with another kind of tattoo or figure out how to get it removed. I'm not hating on your relationship, I want your love to last, but I think you should wait until she is your legal wife before you write her name into your skin.

At the end of the day, getting a tattoo remains your choice. I just want you to understand that these tattoo choices can affect your future family, limit your opportunities in the job market and limit your business earning potential as a business owner

Starting A Business

I know your guardian stresses getting a good education by graduating from college. She or he wants you to have the best chance at getting a great job so you will be able to take care of your family. I do agree that you should learn all that you can. If your family can afford to send you to college or you are able to secure scholarships, you should attend and get that degree. If you do attend college, I think you should get a minor degree in business. I know most people wouldn't mind owning a business. However, the majority of them will never even try to start one. Folks usually get their degrees and go look for a job.

I just know getting a high paying job isn't always guaranteed even if you have a degree. I don't know what the unemployment rate is as you read this book but in black communities, it seems to always be higher than other communities. I want you to learn business because it gives you another option. Understanding how businesses work will even make you a better employee. It will also teach you how to start and operate your own company. I just know the more options you have, the better the chances of you accomplishing your financial goals.

Be mindful that starting a business is hard work. Your success depends on your ability to sell your products and services. You can start a business at any age. Here are some businesses that you can start today with no money or very little money;

1. **Trash dumping (ages 7-10)** : I remember when I was around 8 years old, I used to knock on people's doors and they would pay me to dump their trash. I made a few quarters up to a $1 back then. (Hopefully, you can get paid more than that nowadays) This type of job may not be ideal for a teen but for someone younger it can be a little money in your pocket. I used to live in an apartment building with 30 apartments and I would knock on a lot of those doors. Many people would tell me no, but I would keep knocking until I received a "yes". The more yeses I received, the more money I was able to make. I would increase how much I could earn by asking them if they wanted me to go to the store for them. They would usually pay me around $1 to go to the store. So I

could make $1.00-$10.00 depending on how many yeses I receive.

2. **Carrying Bags at the grocery store (ages 9 and up)**: I used to carry people's bags from the grocery cart to the backseat or the trunk of their car. No long distance walking. Just lifting out of the cart and sitting them down in the car. They would pay me around $1. Depending on how many yeses I got, I could go home with lunch money for a week.

3. **Landscaping (ages 10 & up):** Cutting grass during the fall and summer can make $100s to millions. Let's start small. Someone allows you to borrow their lawnmower and you knock on 5 people's doors on one block and they pay you $25 to mow their lawns. That's $125! I would suggest that you sell them on allowing you to cut their grass every two weeks to three weeks to keep the grass low. If you are able to get them to agree to that, you are guaranteed $125 every two to three weeks. And if you worked on 5 houses a day, you will make $125 in one day. That's good money where you don't

have to worry about the police trying to arrest you or someone shooting you in the head for being in a gang. when the fall comes, you can go to those same customers or new customers and make $25 or more to rake their leaves every week or every couple of weeks. In the winter you can make $30 and up to shovel out their walkway or driveway. You can probably make an additional $20 to shovel out their car and double that if they have more than one car! At a minimum you can make $30 for snow shoveling. You can do this every year for the rest of your life. You can also hire some of your friends and pay them as well The more people you have on your team means the more customers you can service. More customers mean more money.

4. **Washing Cars (ages 10 & up):** Throughout the spring and the summer you can wash people's cars for about $10-20. You can start this business by making a cardboard sign. You can find the sign in the back of a store or ask a store owner for an empty box. You take a marker and write: Car Wash or if a

self -service car wash is near your house, you can hang around the car wash and ask people when they pull up if you can wash their car for them. You can also ask people in your neighborhood.

5. **Visual Artists/Painters (10 & up)**: If you can draw really well, you can sell your artwork in front of your house, online or at public venues. You will need art supplies and canvass. You can sell your artwork for whatever price that people are willing to pay for it. However, I would start with a small or set price like $10. This price can go up depending on how much you are selling. Also, if you are good with creating flyers and notecards online, you can sell them for $40 and up. You can promote your work on social media platforms and sites that allow people to sell items.

6. **Poets/Singers/Rappers 10 & up:** If you are a wordsmith and you have a computer with a recorder on it, you can record your work and sell it online through social media and other platforms. You can sell one poem or song for

$1 to $10 for a whole album. You can also burn CDs from your computer and sell them to people at grocery stores or places where a lot of people go. You can also go to Open Mics and perform live and sell your product at these places. You may even get booked to perform at someone's event and they pay you way more money. You can increase your income by selling the lyrics of your work from $3-$10 a piece.

These are just a few of my suggestions on the kind of businesses you can start with no money or very little money. If you are under the age of 13, I am suggesting that you don't try any of these businesses by yourself. You can do them with a group of friends so you all can keep each other safe or do it with an adult. For my artists, I have a book entitled, Your Art Is Your Empire. It teaches how to protect and market your art. Visit my website at lamontcarey.com or order it on Amazon.com

I'm hoping the experiences I shared with you causes you to think before you act. Just remember that your choices play a major role in what kind of life you live and what kind of man you become. Where you were born doesn't dictate who you will ever be. Choose Life and make Success as your only option.

Other works by Lamont Carey:

THE HILL. Follow Sherman as he begins serving his prison sentence at Lorton Correctional Compound. This complex houses some of the deadliest men in the world. It's a penitentiary so dangerous that other maximum- security prisoners don't wanna go. Sherman made some bad choices in his life. Now he will either live or die from the consequences.

THE WALL is the sequel to the book THE HILL. It takes you to a prison more deadly and sinister than THE HILL. Real Gangsters have been known to scream behind...THE WALL. No one is safe. There are no leaders. Everyone is a killer.

Reach Into My Darkness is a collection of poems that focus on youth issues. Teachers are using this book to get students to express themselves, to think outside of the box and become better decision-makers. It touches on diverse issues that include bullying, peer pressure and education.

Your Art Is Your Empire is a guide for artists who want to turn their dreams into a business. The book covers legal business structures, taxes, marketing material, creating bio, creating your first product and more!

Lamont Carey's award winning CD containing such hits as "I Can't Read", "Confidence", "I Hate This Place", "She Says She Loves Me", and ten other electrifying spokenword pieces. Digital files are available for sale on itunes, CD Baby, amazon and more.

Lamont Carey is an international award-winning spoken word artist, filmmaker, playwright, actor and motivational speaker. To make booking arrangements for speaking or performance engagements for your group, students, prisoners, employees, conferences, or at any other event you are having worldwide, contact LaCarey Enterprises, LLC:

lacareyentertainment@yahoo.com

You may visit the website at:
www.lacareyentertainment.com

Send fan mail to:
LaCarey Entertainment, LLC P.O. Box 64256
Washington, DC 20029

BOOK CHARGING CARD

Accession No. _____ Call No. _____

Author _____

Title _____

Borrower's Name

CPSIA information can be obt___
at www.ICGtesting.com
Printed in the USA
BVOW03s0916290717

490178BV00008E